St. Thérèse of Lisieux

St. Thérèse of Lisieux
A Transformation in Christ

Thomas Keating

Lantern Books
A Division of Booklight Inc.

2001
Lantern Books
One Union Square West, Suite 201
New York, NY 10003

© St. Benedict's Monastery, Snowmass, CO 2001

Scripture texts used in this work are taken from the *New Revised
Standard Version Bible*, copyright 1989, Division of Christian
Education of the National Council of Churches of Christ in the
United States of America.

Printed in the United States of America

Library of Congress Cataloging-in-Publication Data

Keating, Thomas
    St. Thérèse of Lisieux : Transformation in Christ / Thomas
Keating
        p. cm.
    Includes bibliographical references.
    ISBN 1-930051-20-4 (alk. paper)
    1. Jesus Christ—Parables 2. Thérèse of Lisieux, Saint,
1873–1897—Contributions in interpretation of the parables of
Jesus. I. Title

BT375.2.K384 2001
282'.092—dc21

                                    00-047821

❊ *Contents* ❊

Foreword: The Life of St. Thérèse of Lisieux 1

Introduction 5

1: The Publican and the Pharisee 7

2: The Parable of the Mustard Seed 15

3: The Parable of the Leaven 21

4: The Parable of the Barren Fig Tree 39

5: The Parable of the Good Samaritan 49

6: The Parable of the Prodigal Son 55

Chronology of the life of St. Thérèse of Lisieux 61

Bibliography 67

v

❈ *Foreword* ❈
The Life of St. Thérèse of Lisieux

THÉRÈSE MARTIN WAS BORN IN Alençon, France on Thursday, January 2 1873. She was one of nine children—of which only five daughters survived. Her father, Louis, was a watchmaker and jeweler and her mother, Zelie, a lacemaker. Both had planned to enter the religious life before they were married.

Thérèse lost her beloved mother in 1877 to breast cancer and, by her own account, grew into a strong-willed and somewhat spoiled child. When she was nine years old, in 1882, her "second Mama"—her older sister Pauline—joined the Carmel of Lisieux, leaving Thérèse bereft once more. Always sickly and fragile, Thérèse was cured from a life-threatening illness when she was ten years old through a vision of the smile of the Blessed Virgin Mary. In 1886, Thérèse's sister Marie entered the Carmel of Lisieux (her sister Léonie was to join the Poor Clares). Thérèse began to feel the call herself and the following year was given permission by her father to enter Carmel.

Before she could enter Carmel, however, she had to overcome more obstacles. The superior of the Carmelite convent refused to accept Thérèse into the order because she was so young. Thérèse took the matter to the local bishop, who likewise refused to allow it. Finally, Thérèse, her sister Céline, and her father went on pilgrimage to Rome, where Thérèse managed to obtain an audience with Pope Leo XIII and begged him to allow her to join the Carmelites. The Pope was impressed with her courage and spirit, but would not intervene, referring Thérèse to the superior of the convent of Lisieux. Thérèse entered Lisieux Carmel on April 9, 1888 at the age of fifteen.

A few years after her entrance, Thérèse's father suffered a series of strokes that destroyed his mental and physical health and, in 1892, Louis Martin returned from Caen an invalid in the care of his late wife's family. (He was to die in July 1894.)

Thérèse, who had made profession of final vows in September 1890, was allowed to remain in the novitiate in 1893 and wrote her first dramatic piece (on Joan of Arc) in January 1894. In September her sister Céline entered Lisieux Carmel, followed a year later by her cousin Marie Guérin. During this period, Thérèse began writing the manuscripts that were to become her autobiography, which was called *Story of a Soul*.

In April 1896 she spat up blood for the first time and fell seriously ill at the same time a year later. She was transferred to the monastery infirmary on July 8, 1897. She died on Thursday, September 30 and was buried in the Lisieux cemetery.

A year after her death, two thousand copies of *Story of a Soul* were printed and the book became immediately popular. Thérèse was beatified by Pius XI in 1923 and canonized two years later. In 1980, John Paul II made a pilgrimage to Lisieux and later declared Thérèse a Doctor of the Church.

❊ *Introduction* ❊

THIS TINY BOOK IS A TASTE OF THE spiritual wisdom St. Thérèse of Lisieux and how it resonates with the parables of Jesus and their relationship to the spiritual journey. It was written in honor of Thérèse's becoming the third woman Doctor of the Church and as a token of my immense gratitude for her inspiration in starting and sustaining me on the path of Christian contemplation. I rely heavily on the scholarship of Bernard Brandon Scott and his book, *Here Then the Parable* (Fortress Press, 1989), on which I base these reflections.

St. Thérèse in my view is the key figure in the recovery of the contemplative dimension of the Gospel in our time—a process that is desperately needed in the Christian community and is only just beginning to take root. Thérèse manifests an extraordinary penetration into the heart of Jesus' teaching about the kingdom of God, as well as a precise program for bringing it into daily life. She understood and participated profoundy in Jesus' experience of the Ultimate Reality as Abba, a tender and loving word for Father.

❋ *Chapter One* ❋
The Publican and the Pharisee

L ET US FIRST ENTER THE MYSTERIOUS and astonishing world of Jesus' parables and then show what an extraordinary insight Thérèse had into those enigmatic stories. Using Thérèse's teaching as a guide, my first reflection is distilled from the parable of the Publican and the Pharisee. Usually interpreted as an example of pride and humility, this parable has quite a different meaning once we grasp the context in which the hearers were listening to the story.

Two people went up to the temple to pray, one a Pharisee and the other a tax collector. The Pharisee, standing by himself, was praying thus: "God, I thank you that I am not like other people: thieves, rogues, adulterers, or even like this tax collector. I fast twice a week; I give a tenth of all my income." But the tax collector, standing far off, would not even look up to heaven, but was beating his breast and saying: "God, be merciful to me, a sinner!" I tell you, this man went down to his home justified rather than the other. (Luke 18:10–14)

In this parable, the Pharisee is standing in the Temple and recounting his good deeds to the Lord during prayer. Recounting good deeds was not considered an expression of pride in those days, but the normal way that Pharisees prayed. It was an expression of their social status as holy men praying in a holy place. In the popular mind, holiness was associated with sacred places and sacred times.

In this parable, the Pharisee represents someone who was an insider in the social structure of the culture. People at that time paid a lot of attention to demarcating who was inside the social structure and acceptable and who was outside and unacceptable. In our times, this demarcation is expressed in racial and ethnic prejudices, and has manifested itself on a monumental scale in the horrors we have witnessed in Rwanda and the former Yugoslavia.

The tax collector in the parable is from the secular world. He stands outside the sacred precincts of the Temple and prays simply: "God, be merciful to me, a sinner!" The tax collector was just doing what he was supposed to do in that religious culture, which was to stay outside the sacred place. A sharp distinction is thus made between those who belong to the sacred elite and those who come from ordinary life.

The conclusion of the parable probably seemed unbelievable to those who were hearing it for the first time. Jesus states that the tax collector went back to his home justified—that is, all his sins were forgiven—but that the Pharisee did not! That means that sacred places are not essential for someone to be able to enter the Kingdom of God. In Jesus' teaching, the sacred place is where you are. It is ordinary, daily life.

* * *

The idea that the sacred place is right where you are is a revolution in the popular concept of the sacred. There are places such as churches and shrines where we are spiritually renewed, where we hear the word of God, and where we may have spiritual experiences. But they are not the usual places where transformation takes place, according to this parable.

Our reactions to daily life are the gauge of the depth of our prayer and the empowerment that it provides. An obvious question following from this would be: Why do people enter monasteries or the religius life if the backyard is just as sacred as the cloister? The answer is that it is only appropriate if one has a genuine attraction to religious life indicating that God wants it to be everyday life for us—in other words, if to live in a monastery is our particular vocation.

For most people, daily life in the secular world is the place where transformation in Christ is worked out. Like the Pharisee, one can be in religious life and not be transformed. So, what is it that makes the difference between the daily transformed life and the religious untransformed life? It is the hidden action of the Kingdom of God that works not so much through external circumstances as through a radical change in our attitudes. This is what transformation is. It is not going on pilgrimage or entering a special state of life. It is how we live where we are and what we do with those circumstances.

The ordinary circumstances of daily life bring back the same faults, the same temptations, the same routines, and often the sense of going nowhere! But "nowhere" is where the Kingdom of God is most active. Grace and daily life are always in dialogue and sometimes in a state of war. There is a struggle to figure out what God is saying in the events and circumstances of daily life and how everyday life is meant to transform us.

What Thérèse called the "Little Way" is quite simply the circumstances of everyday life and what we do with them. The role of Centering Prayer or some similar method is to bring us into daily contact with God and especially into a disposition of attentiveness to his word in scripture and to his silent word within us. Listening to God in silent, loving attentiveness, enables us to let go of our preconceptions and over-identification with the events of daily life, which tends to dominate our emotional reactions rather than invite our free response.

Events and people dominate us when our emotional reactions to them are the center of our attention and our thoughts. "How can people do this to me? Am I going to lose my job? Why are the children misbehaving? What am I going to do about mother and father now that they are ready for a nursing home?"

With such reflections buzzing in our heads, how do we listen to what the Spirit is saying and act out of divine love? "Everything is a grace" was one of Thérèse's favorite sayings—a saying that while right to the point, is still terribly hard to grasp. How, we may ask can *everything* be a grace? To grasp this insight, we must look at another parable that Thérèse understood to the depths: the parable of the mustard seed.

❈ Chapter Two ❈
The Parable of the Mustard Seed

He said therefore: "What is the Kingdom of God like? And to what shall I compare it? It is like a mustard seed that someone took and sowed in the garden; it grew and became a tree, and the birds of the air made nests in its branches." (Luke 13:18–19)

A MUSTARD SEED IS SOWN IN A GARDEN. The mustard seed was proverbially the smallest of all seeds. It grew into a bush. Jesus apparently did not explain this parable. The meaning that I am sharing with you does not have to be yours—indeed, you may prefer another meaning. But I would urge you at least to consider this one, since Thérèse took it very much to heart.

To understand the parable in the context of the times, we need to realize that the Kingdom of God for the Israelite community of that period held special connotations. One of these was the hope of a vindictive triumph over the Roman Empire which had been oppressing the nation for decades. The people were living under the boot of an alien power that disregarded the values of their religion and kept them in oppressive circumstances. They were asking: "How can we be the chosen people according to the Torah, especially loved by God, and yet still be living in such miserable circumstances? How can we reconcile our faith in God's sovereignty and power and accept the fact that he does nothing to change the situation?"

This is one of the great questions that faith is confronted with. How can we experience so much negativity in our lives and yet go on believing that a loving God is in charge of everything? Why doesn't God change things? We keep pounding on the door of heaven with our petitions and there doesn't seem to be anybody home. God seems to ignore us.

Job asked similar questions, according to the famous Old Testament story, when he had his own personal difficulties with God. The parable of the mustard seed is Jesus' response to this problem. In Luke's version of the parable, the seed grows into a tree. Perhaps Luke's reasoning was that the mustard seed, if it was to be a symbol of the Kingdom of God, had to grow into something significant. In actual fact, mustard seeds do not grow into trees. They do not grow into cedars of Lebanon, which could reach to three hundred feet in height and hold a lot of birds.

For the listeners to Jesus' parable, a mustard seed could only grow into a small bush—not more than four feet high and only a few birds would be able to make a bedraggled nest in its branches. As a symbol, therefore, the mustard seed is the reverse of what the Israelites at the time had in mind when they envisaged the Kingdom of God. They believed that, through Israel, God would establish his sovereignty and rule over all the nations of the world. Yet, the parable clearly states that the Kingdom of God has nothing to do with a vindictive triumph over one's enemies or wordly success. What this parable clearly implies is that, if you think that your church, your nation, or your ethnic group is going to be delivered by God, and enjoy a magnificent triumph—or if you expect that the world is going to be converted to Jesus Christ—you are mistaken; it isn't going to happen. What the Gospel is interested in is you. Not what you can *do*; just plain you.

St. Thérèse writes:

Holiness does not consist in this or that practice but in a disposition of heart [notice the shift from externals to internals] which remains always humble and little in God's arms, but trusting to audacity in the Father's goodness.

That is what St. Thérèse meant when she talked about the way of spiritual childhood. This is what Jesus meant when he said: "Truly I tell you, unless you change and become like children, you will never enter the kingdom of heaven." (Matt.18:3). He was thinking of a good family, where the children can fully trust their parents.

❖ Chapter Three ❖
The Parable of the Leaven

THERE IS ANOTHER PARABLE THAT GOES even farther. (Jesus' teaching builds up in intensity and depth as he goes along.) This is the parable of the leaven hidden in the dough. This parable is exactly the same in theGospels of Matthew and Luke and goes like this:

> *The Kingdom of God is like yeast that a woman took and mixed in with three measures of flour until all of it was leavened. (Matt. 13:33)*

In Jesus' time, leaven was a lively symbol of corruption. Leaven was made by allowing a piece of bread to rot in a dark, damp place until it stank. Then you put the rotten bread in the dough until the dough was permeated by it. The juxtaposition of leavened and unleavened bread was another way in which the religious society of the time expressed the importance of separating the sacred from the secular, the feast day from everyday life.

The woman in the parable takes three measures of flour. This amount is enough to feed about fifty people—so, we are not talking about a modest meal that the woman is preparing; we're talking about enough to feed a small army! Three measures of flour are the same measure that we hear about in Genesis, when Sarah provides bread at Abraham's request for the three angelic visitors at the Oaks of Mamre. Thus in the minds of the hearers of the parable, the number suggests that a special revelation of God is taking place.

Yet, in the parable, instead of being an epiphany of holiness, the batch of leavened bread becomes a revelation of corruption. As a result, the hearers of the parable would have been left wondering: "Is this man saying that good is evil? How can he propose that leaven, especially after it leavens a whole mass of dough, is a revelation of the Kingdom of God? He should say just the opposite." If leavened bread, as we have seen, was the popular symbol of corruption, fifty loaves must have suggested corruption on a monumental scale.

* * *

The parable clearly raises the question: How do we know what is good and what is evil? Such a question presupposes that one has a value system. And it is our value system that Jesus is confronting in this parable: we may need to doubt the reliability of what we feel is good and evil. As we have seen, the Kingdom of God is not limited to sacred places. God feels free to come to us in any guise whatsoever. The Kingdom of God is present is daily life when events that we consider disasters occur. God is never absent—it is just our belief system that makes us think that God could not be present when things, according to our judgement, go wrong.

The Parable of the Leaven suggests that God is never more present than when things are going wrong. The leaven, symbol of what we regard as evil for us, could be physical, mental, or moral disabilities in us or in those we love. Jesus teaches that the Kingdom of God is present there; just how it is present is what we have to figure out.

This is the challenge of everyday life. God is always there, but everything in us may say: "God can't be here." Or we may ask, "If God is all merciful and all powerful, why is he allowing this to happen to me?" As symbolized by the enormous batch of leavened bread, what we may be feeling is massive corruption! "Where is Jesus?" we may ask? "Where is God, who is always saying how much he loves me and protects me? God…. Do something!"

What God is looking for is not to change situations that seem horrendously destructive or corrupt. He is hoping to change *us*. Changing us may sometimes require disasters. We have preconceived ideas that have never been challenged, mindsets that we have brought with us from early childhood or picked up along the way. Most, if not all, of these values are not those of the Gospel! God invites us to change them; and, if we cannot do it on our own, he provides us with circumstances that may seem to us insurmountable or overwhelming.

St. Thérèse had this kind of trouble. First, she developed tuberculosis that grew worse as her life in the Lisieux Carmel convent unfolded. She was virtually bedridden during the last year of her life. She could not praise God at the divine office anymore; she could not attend daily Mass; she could not even think of heaven that had previously been so great a consolation for her. Heaven, she felt, was closed to her—as if there were an iron curtain in front of it whenever she tried to think about it. In other words, her painful disease and her spiritual purification were going on at the same time.

Sometimes three or four corruptions are going on at the same time! You may have physical, mental, moral and spiritual evils going on all at once. When people undergo these things, they need all the support we can give them because they are really hurting. But, we should ask, is it only physical, mental, moral, or spiritual corruption that we feel? Is the experience of intense suffering the only reality?

Christ's passion, death, and resurrection are being worked out in us through the events of daily life, that is, through what happens. His resurrection is at the bottom of whatever the pile of corruption may be, and in due time it will emerge. The cross and resurrection are two sides of the same reality. While we sometimes experience one more than the other, in the mature Christian they come together. It does not matter which is predominant, because the other is always present.

Let us look at the situation from God's point of view. Here is God, sending into the world his only Son, who, as St. Paul says, "became sin for us." In other words, Jesus took upon himself all the consequences of our sinfulness on the cross. The chief consequences are: the sense of God's absence, the sense of alienation from God, and, at times, even the feeling of rejection by God.

We are identified with Christ less by our virtues than by our sins. It is our sinfulness and weakness that Christ has taken upon himself; all the consequences of personal sin, symbolized by his descent into hell. The Greek Orthodox liturgy of Holy Saturday affirms that Christ truly descended into the place of the damned.

Hell is primarily a state of mind, a state of soul, a state characterized by total alienation from God— so total that one does not even want to have it changed! Hell exists even in this life for people who endure unbearable mental suffering. One who is experiencing total alienation from God cannot think of anything else. One is totally immersed in one's sense of desolation, loneliness, and reprobation. This is precisely the extent to which Christ has identified with us. By identifying with all the consequences of our sins and taking the suffering of the whole of humanity into himself, Christ descended into that state of consciousness that corresponds to hell—or more exactly, *is* hell.

To participate in that kind of absence or alienation from God is the most powerful and mature identity with Jesus that one can come to in the Christian life. That is why it is a mistake to think of our spiritual journey as an ascent to glory or as a magic carpet to bliss. It is rather the increasing capacity to enter into Christ's passion, death, descent into hell, and resurrection. That is the greatest participation in Christ's Paschal Mystery, and hence the foundation for the greatest participation in his resurrection. It is also the greatest participation in the redemption of the world, which is the great project that Jesus initiated and achieved in his own humanity and now invites us to share. Therese accepted this invitation with her whole heart, writing toward the end of her life: "Suffering through love is the one thing that seems desirable to me in this vale of tears."

* * *

Sometimes everyday life may involve not just routine discomfort and distress, but physical or mental disaster. In Thérèse's case, her father developed a mental illness after she entered the convent. After having sent four daughters, including his favorite one, to the convent, it is no wonder he suffered a mental breakdown. Thérèse's sister Céline was at home taking care of him and he could come to the convent only rarely. It was an excruciating trial for Thérèse because she felt so close to him. She writes in her letters to Céline that together they are making giant steps in the love of God by accepting the situation, living with it, and praising God for the mysterious work he is doing.

We can be sure that even mental illness is part of God's plan. God may be using that illness for a person's sanctification, perhaps much more than we realize. Some people who suffer mental difficulties may be closer to God than others, because of the intensity of their pain. If you have ever known anybody who suffered from serious mental illness or schizophrenia, you will understand what I am talking about. One feels utterly powerless in the face of poignant human tragedies. And yet we are asked to believe that the Kingdom of God is right there in the midst of them.

God is present in physical illness as well. The Kingdom is especially active when someone has a physical disability. It is also very active, as Jesus suggests, in the marginalized people of a particular society. God's identification with the outcasts of society is exemplified by the occasions when Jesus sat down to eat with public sinners.

In the Palestinian culture of the time, to eat with someone was to identify with his or her state of life or condition. To the horror of his disciples and certainly of the Pharisees, Jesus ate with sinners in public. Indeed, it would seem from the Gospels, that he ate with them more often than he did with "respectable" people.

While not approving of their behavior, Jesus was identifying with the emotional wounds they were suffering from the consequences of their sins or the compulsive drives within them. In this parable

Jesus asks the question: "Who are you to judge anyone?" Certainly, we are not judges, because, to be qualified, a judge needs to have all the facts and to be appointed by some authority. We do not have all the facts and nobody has appointed us to judge anyone.

Thérèse worked very hard to practice the wisdom sayings of Jesus in the Sermon on the Mount. She started by reaching out to others in little things because she saw God in them. Thérèse was always thinking of other people and doing little favors for them, though in a way that did not become annoying. As she put it, "But one thing is necessary—to work solely for God and to do nothing for self or for creatures."

When she was a novice, she served an aging sister who had to have help coming to choir from the infirmary. The older sister was a very grumpy old lady and nothing Thérèse did could please her. She would say: "Watch out you don't drop me! You're just a child; be careful!" No matter what

Thérèse did, nothing could satisfy the old Sister. As Thérèse puts it in her autobiography, *Story of a Soul*:

I prayed earnestly for this Sister who had caused me so much struggle.... I tried to do everything I possibly could for her, and when tempted to answer her sharply, I hastened to give her a friendly smile and talk about something else.

Thérèse put up with her complaints day after day. After a year of leading the old nun to vespers every day and of being berated at almost every step, Therese heard these words from the old nun: "Whenever we meet, you give me such a gracious smile. What is it that you find so attractive in me?" Thérèse does not record what she said in response, but she does write about what she felt: "What attracted me? It was Jesus hidden in the depths of her soul, Jesus who makes attractive even what is most bitter."

At other times, far from reaching out to people, Thérèse withdrew, because, she knew that it if she reached out, she might have punched the other person in the nose! When we are annoyed with someone and want to say a harsh word to put them in their place, or share with them a bit of gossip that would hurt them, true reaching out might mean beating a hasty retreat! One time, Thérèse felt her emotions building up and she felt that she would say something that would hurt someone and that if she stayed another moment the words would come out. Claiming that she had something very important to do in the sacristy, she literally ran away and sat down on the stairs in the sacristy with her heart beating like mad:

I simply longed to defend myself, but happily I had a bright idea. I knew I would certainly lose my peace of mind if I tried to justify myself. I knew too that I was not virtuous enough to remain silent in the face of this accusation. There was only one way out—I must run away. No sooner thought than done; I fled!...but my heart was beating so violently that I could not go very far, and I sat down on the stairs to enjoy quietly the fruits of my victory.

In her autobiography, Thérèse adds that this modest triumph over her emotional compulsions was "a strange kind of bravery, but it was better than exposing myself to certain defeat!"

Sometimes our best way of dealing with emotions when they are out of hand is to beat a hasty retreat. This is not to give up the war. It is just a strategic move to re-gather our forces and to come back to the job of self-denial when we are in a better disposition. Notice the carefulness and the resoluteness with which Thérèse pursued all the manifestations of the false self within her, doing what she could to resist them.

To reach out against her natural inclination in order to help someone is what Thérèse meant by her Little Way. She described it as "capturing Jesus by caresses." She made progress in dismantling the false self not by experiencing great spiritual consolations, but by the daily practice of letting go of selfish inclinations, or rather by welcoming them, because they showed her the depths of her own weakness and feebleness. That is why she could say: "Even if I had on my conscience every conceivable crime, I would lose nothing of my confidence." Why? Because she had firm faith that Jesus in his passion and death had taken every consequence of sin upon himself, and then rose from the dead, taking with him all who have accepted his invitation to follow him. To repeat Thérèse's conviction:

Even if I had on my conscience every conceivable sin, I would lose nothing of my confidence. My heart overflowing with love, I would throw myself into the arms of the Father, and I am certain that I would be warmly received.

This is one of the greatest insights of all time into the nature of God and of our relationship with him.

* * *

The truth is, as Thérèse affirmed, that God is all-powerful and all-merciful. Therefore, "we can never have too much confidence in him." On the contrary, our audacity in trusting God rather than our hesitations due to false humility is the path to divine union. Our interior misgivings make that leap of trust difficult unless we keep working at the Little Way. If we do, we begin to notice that our attitudes toward events and people are changing. We no longer project our human expectations on God or harbor preconceived ideas about how God should proceed.

You can be sure that whatever you think is the way to go to God, it is not. Even if you believe you are correct and can find spiritual authors to support you, just because you *think* you are on the right road, God will find another road that is just as good, so you won't cling to the self-satisfying certitude that you are right. Our preconceptions, biases, and false value systems are significant hindrances. In Thérèse's view, openness to God coming to us in daily life through events and people is a most important disposition to cultivate.

❈ *Chapter Four* ❈
The Parable of the Barren Fig Tree

A man had a fig tree planted in his vineyard; and he came looking for fruit on it and found none. So he said to the gardener: "See here! For three years I have come looking for fruit on this fig tree, and still I find none. Cut it down! Why should it be wasting the soil?" He replied: "Sir, let it alone for one more year, until I dig around it and put some manure on it. If it bear fruit next year, well and good; but if not, you can cut it down." (Luke 13:6–9)

I N THIS PARABLE, THE HOUSEHOLDER TELLS the gardener to cut the tree down and the gardener responds by pleading for a year's reprieve. What could this mean? It seems to me that this parable offers a powerful representation of how we experience daily life when we are committed to the spiritual journey—whether we are trying to take on the mind of Christ, to put into effect the values of the Gospel, or to manifest the fruits of the Spirit—charity, joy, peace, patience, meekness, goodness, gentleness, self-control, and fidelity.

Manure means dung, of course—a very down-to-earth term. The term "dung," and particularly the product, has a certain pungency. Yet, because of the rich nutrients found there, trees like dung. Dung is the symbol of our experience of daily life and of our constantly recurring faults. The dung represents our experience of daily prayer as one of going nowhere, or even the inability to pray at all, and of the endless flow of unwanted thoughts. Dung also represents the psychological experience of how disagreeable daily life often is, and that nothing we do really helps to improve the situation. Turning on the television or making a phone call may give us a brief respite, but then we are back in the same old emotional hole we were in before. Indeed, we may be further in the hole than we were before. The means we normally use to assuage the pain of daily life are not the best way to proceed.

The right way is to shovel the dung around the tree—that is, to keep putting up with one's faults and still go on trusting in God. Of course, all the manure in the world is not going to change that tree. But if you keep shoveling, at some point God is going to give life to that tree—not because of the dung, but because you kept trying, and God was so touched that he gave life to the tree anyway. Therese comments on this subject, "I experience a lively joy not only in being judged imperfect, but above all, when I *feel* that I am. That joy is sweeter to me than all compliments, which really only weary me."

* * *

Thérèse expressed her insight into this parable in her example of an elevator:

We live in the age of inventions now, and the wealthy no longer have to take the trouble to climb the stairs; they take an elevator. That is what I must find, *an elevator* to take me straight up to Jesus, because I am too little to climb the steep stairway of perfection. So, I searched the Scriptures for some hint of my desired *elevator*, until I came upon these words from the lips of Eternal Wisdom: *"Whosoever is a little one, let him come to Me."* (Prov. 9:4). I went closer to God, feeling sure that I was on the right path, but as I wanted to know what He would do to a "little one," I continued my search. This is what I found: *"You shall be carried at the breasts and upon the knees, as one whom the mother caresseth, so will I comfort you."* (Is. 66:12,13). My heart had never been moved by such tender and consoling words before! [italics in the original]

Somebody once asked Thérèse how to reach holiness, and her answer was as follows. Think of a tiny child at the bottom of a long staircase with her beloved father at the top. This little child is only eighteen months old and the stairs are steep and long. The child is reaching out her hands to her father to come and pick her up. The father is at the top of the stairs saying: "Come on! Come on!" All though the Gospel, we get the same invitation: "Come and be transformed, forget your faults, forget your sins. Just be with me in the present moment and I will take care of you." But because we are not like little children, we don't hear the reassurance.

The child keeps raising her tiny foot, but even with her greatest efforts there is no chance of getting to the first step because her legs are too short. The child keeps raising one tiny foot and then the other, all to no avail. There is no chance at all she is going to negotiate even the first step. Her father keeps on calling her with immense tenderness: "Come on! Come on! I'm waiting for you!" She keeps trying and trying. In other words, the child keeps shoveling the manure—accepting her weakness and her inability to make any progress. But she does not give up even though the task is impossible.

Thérèse says that if the child keeps up her helpless efforts, the Father himself, because of his great love, will not be able to stand the situation anymore and will come rushing down the stairs, gather her into his arms, and carry her to the top of the stairs. Thérèse says that this is how she got where she was in the spiritual life: not by any efforts of her own, but by the infinite mercy and tenderness of God.

This is why Thérèse's insight into the Gospel is so great a contribution to spiritual renewal in our time, especially to the renewal of the contemplative life, which is the way of spirtual childhood—that is, of listening to God, waiting, trying, trusting, and turning ourselves over to God. This way means refusing to listen to our commentaries that say we are not getting anywhere, or that we will never make it. Or, to be more specific, it means not complaining that we cannot negotiate the spiritual life because we are having problems in our marriage, business, professional life, or with our children, money, or some addiction.

The difficulties just listed may be very real, and I do not want to minimize them. But God is using these difficulties to give us the Kingdom, and the coming of the Kingdom is conditioned only by our consent and acceptance of the situation. One may try to change the situation, but always with detachment from the results.

The Kingdom is most powerful where we least expect to find it. God does not take away our problems and trials but rather joins us in them. Such is the profound meaning of the Incarnation: God becoming a human being. The Kingdom will manifest itself, not because of our efforts to keep trying, *even when all effort seems hopeless*, but because God loves us so much that God won't be able to stand seeing us struggle and always failing. God will do the impossible. He will give us a new attitude toward suffering. Such is the heart of the Christian *ascesis*, or self-discipline, and the mystery of transformation. It is the meaning of the Gospel as Thérèse perceived it.

Is this program too hard? Everyone can love and everyone can suffer: that is all we need. It gets a little uncomfortable now and then, but it also perks up every now and then. And it does not matter whether there is discomfort or pleasure, because God is fully present at all times! Whatever psychological trauma or difficulty we experience—even when we are the cause of our own suffering—that trauma or event is the way God alerts us to the fact that we need to let go of something to which we are overly attached. Some preconceived idea or prejudice is putting us into a straight jacket. The Little Way is the path of liberation from our false self with its over-identification with our emotional programs for happiness and our cultural conditioning.

* * *

Here is an important distinction. We have feelings, but we are not our feelings. Indeed, we should not say, "I'm angry" or "I'm in despair." We should rather say, "I have angry feelings," or "I have feelings of despair." We can do something about these feelings once we do not identify with them. We can choose what to do with them. Remembering the distinction between "having feelings" and "being" our feelings allows us to change our attitude and look more kindly upon our feebleness and failings. Therese writes, "I accept all for the love of God, even the most extravagant thoughts that come to my mind and intrude themselves upon me."

While it is important for us to work on our addictions—if not for ourselves, then at least for the sake of other people—it is vital to know that only God can deliver us. Freedom usually comes only after a long wait—not because God wants to keep us waiting, but because we are not ready to be healed. We have first to hit bottom and know experientially that we cannot do it ourselves. Then God's grace can provide the healing. External disciplines can be harmful if we put too much confidence in them. We may think that if we do certain things we will force God to help us. But God responds only to love. It is a relationship. It was in the fullness of that relationship that Thérèse died. Her last words were what her life had become: an act of love, "Oh my God, I love you!"

❈ Chapter Five ❈
The Parable of the Good Samaritan

A man was going down from Jerusalem to Jericho, and fell into the hands of robbers, who stripped him, beat him, and went away, leaving him half dead. Now by chance a priest was going down that road; and when he saw him, he passed by on the other side. So likewise a Levite, when he came to the place and saw him, passed by on the other side. But a Samaritan while traveling came near him; and when he saw him, he was moved with pity. He went to him and bandaged his wounds, having poured oil and wine on them. Then he put him on his own animal, brought him to an inn, and took care of him. The next day he took out two denarii, gave them to the innkeeper, and said: "Take care of him; and when I come back, I will repay you whatever more you spend." Which of these three, do you think, was a neighbor to the man who fell into the hands of the robbers? He said: "The one who showed him mercy." Jesus said to him: "Go and do likewise." (Luke 10:30–37)

L IKE THE OTHER PARABLES I HAVE discussed in this book, this parable also describes the social map of Israel. We find several people on a journey to Jericho, one of whom gets beaten up. A priest and a Levite make the same journey and pass by the wounded man. The third person would normally be a layperson in the Israelite social structure. The story is very cleverly put together. It builds on the triad that was so familiar to people in the social structure of the time:

that is, priest, Levite, and layperson. We have to remember, too, that Samaritans were regarded as mortal enemies of the Jewish nation and apostates from the Jewish religion as well. For the listeners, there could hardly be a more precise image of moral corruption coming down the road than a Samaritan.

Sure enough, in Jesus' parable, along comes a Samaritan. The hearers probably think that the Samaritan will just finish off the poor man by the side of the road. Instead, the Samaritan begins to show all kinds of mercy. The story obviously undermines the social presuppositions of that period in Palestinian society. The message is clear that whoever you think is your enemy may be your greatest friend. Even more significantly, the parable undermines the easy assumption that we all have regarding what is good and what is evil. The good guy becomes the bad guy and the bad guy the good, leaving some of the listeners to conclude that the story is just unbelievable and to write it off as of no interest. The parable emphasizes that there are no barriers in the Kingdom of heaven. Barriers are things that human beings set up, not God, and, if we do not take down these barriers, they could follow us into the next life.

The parable emphasizes that God is the Father of everyone. There are no elites, no chosen ones, because everybody is chosen in God's plan. God desires all persons to be saved. This idea of God was revolutionary for the people of the time. As we have seen, the popular conception envisaged God as the defender of Israel, as the God of armies, as the God of Mount Sinai, of the sacred and the transcendent. Jesus completely undermines this idea of God.

Thérèse's idea of God was God extending his love to everybody. In the last few months of her life she wrote: "Love fulfills every vocation." We do not have to go to the missions. We do not have to teach catechism. We do not have to do this or that good work. We have to do something—that is, what is at hand and what we can easily do—to minister to the emotional, physical, and spiritual needs of others. Showing kindness, reaching out to those in trouble, and holding the hand of those in sorrow—these works of mercy manifest the Kingdom of God. Thérèse sought to do everything out of love. In her judgment, "To pick up a pin out of love can convert a soul."

Think then of the enormous potentialities of this humble, hidden, but persevering love that consists not in sentiment but in showing love to those who need it. In the circumstances of daily life—in the family, at work or wherever—just keep showing love. We walk down the street, talk with people, work, play. Why not do everything as a way of manifesting God and allowing God in us to reveal his love to everyone? When we go to the movies or to church, or are in a big crowd, why not open our hearts to everybody and surround them with the love of God. Or ask ourselves how we might be reconciled with the members of our family, forgive our enemies, practice the various works of mercy, endure sickness and death out of love for God. In Therese's view, love is all that counts.

❈ *Chapter Six* ❈
The Parable of the Prodigal Son

There was a man who had two sons. The younger of them said to his father: "Father, give me the share of the property that will belong to me." So he divided his property between them. A few days later the younger son gathered all he had and traveled to a distant country, and there he squandered his property in dissolute living. When he had spent everything, a severe famine took place throughout that country, and he began to be in need. So he went and hired himself out to one of the citizens in that country, who sent him to his fields to feed the pigs. He would gladly have filled himself with the pods that the pigs were eating; and no one gave him anything. But when he came to himself he said: "How many of my father's hired hands have bread enough and to spare, but here I am dying of hunger! I will get up and go to my father, and I will say to him: 'Father, I have sinned against heaven and before you; I am no longer worthy to be called your son; treat me like one of your hired hands.' " So he set off and went to his father. But while he was still far off, his father saw him and was filled with compassion; he ran and put his arms around him and kissed him. Then the son said to him: "Father, I have sinned against heaven and before you; I am no longer worthy to be called your son." But the father said to his slaves: "Quickly, bring out a robe—the best one—and put it on him; put a ring on his finger and sandals on his feet. And get the fatted calf and kill it, and let us eat and celebrate; for this son of mine was dead and is alive again; he was lost and is found!" And they began to celebrate.

Now his elder son was in the field; and when he came and approached the house, he heard music and dancing. He called one of the slaves and asked what was going on. He replied: "Your brother has come, and your father has killed the fatted calf, because he has got him back safe and sound." Then he became angry and refused to go in. His father came out and began to plead with him. But he answered his father: "Listen! For all these years I have never disobeyed your command; yet you have never given me even a young goat so that I might celebrate with my friends. But when this son of yours came back, who has devoured your property with prostitutes, you killed the fatted calf for him!" Then the father said to him: "Son, you are always with me, and all that is mine is yours. But we had to celebrate and rejoice, because this brother of yours was dead and has come to life; he was lost and has been found." (Luke 15:11–32)

THERE ARE TWO YOUNG MEN IN THIS story. One is the son who set out for the good life, came to ruin, returned home, and was received without any request for repentance or that he repay the money he had spent, part of which was to take care of his father in his old age.

The other son is one of those self-righteous people who do all the right things but for the wrong reasons. He was looking for the inheritance too, and he felt he had a right to be angry with his brother who had squandered his share. It meant that the eldest son would have to pay for the support of the old man all by himself.

The older son berates his father for his goodness, thus breaking the fourth commandment, which is to honor father and mother. Thus, both sons fail. The father embraces and forgives his wayward son without a word of remonstrance and lovingly remonstrates with the one who was well behaved but bitter and self-righteous. We may suspect that the older son was seeking his own gain by behaving properly in order to guarantee for himself the full inheritance. To remonstrate with self-righteous people is quite a job. The father tries to explain: "My son was lost and is found; we have to rejoice."

The point to emphasize here is that this father, instead of worrying about his honor, which was very important in that culture, throws it away and does not act as the typical patriarchal father. Instead, he acts rather as a mother and forgives both sons. His chief concern is that they live together in peace and harmony.

* * *

The Gospel precept, "To love one another as I have loved you!" is the program that Thérèse tried to carry out on a day-to-day basis. One wonders whether this is not the best program to propose to people—since anybody can do it, because everybody has an everyday life. The Kingdom of God is in everyday life and in what we do with it. We have to keep trusting in God when physical, mental, and emotional difficulties arise for us and those we love. These are occasions to open us to deeper self-knowledge and self-surrender to God.

We may have to struggle with what is most difficult for those sincerely seeking God—the inability to overcome our faults or sins.

As we saw in the Parable of the Leaven, the Kingdom of God is present in the midst of vast corruption. Perhaps what we have to do is to accept the humiliation of not being as good as we would like and to do the best we can, trusting audaciously in the Father's goodness and in the power of divine love to heal the wounds of a lifetime. As Thérèse knew, the experience of divine love is the ultimate healing. No matter what our difficulties are, Thérèse urges us to continue to show love, to build instead of tearing down, and to trust God with boundless confidence. She writes:

> What pleases God is to see me love my poverty and the blind hope I have in his mercy ... Please, understand that to love God, the weaker one is, without desires or virtues, the more apt one is for the operations of that consuming and transforming love.

✳ *Chronology* ✳

1873

Thursday, January 2: Thérèse born in Alençon, France.
Saturday, January 4: Thérèse baptized in Notre-Dame
Church.

1877

Wednesday, August 28: Death of Thérèse's mother, Zélie
Martin, at 12:30 AM.

1882

Monday, October 2: Pauline, her "second Mama," enters
the Carmel of Lisieux.

1883

Sunday, May 13 (Pentecost): Thérèse cured suddenly by the Blessed Virgin's smile.

1886

Friday, October 15: Marie enters Carmel of Lisieux.
Saturday, December 25 (Christmas): grace of "conversion."

1887

Sunday, May 29 (Pentecost): Thérèse receives her father's permission to enter Carmel.
Monday, October 31: Thérèse visits Bishop Hugonin in Bayeux.
Friday, November 4 to Friday, December 2: Thérèse on pilgrimage to Paris, Switzerland, Italy, and Rome.

1888

Monday, April 9 (Annunciation): Thérèse enters Lisieux Carmel.

1889

Thursday, January 10: Thérèse clothed in the religious habit.

1890

Monday, September 8 (Birth of Mary): Thérèse's final profession of vows.

1892

Tuesday, May 10: (After three years at Caen, Louis Martin returns to Lisieux an invalid, in the care of the Guérins.)

Thursday, May 12: Louis Martin's last visit to his Carmelite daughters. His final words to them: "In heaven!"

1893

September: Thérèse obtains permission to remain in novitiate.

1894

January: Thérèse writes her first theatrical work, on Joan of Arc, for the prioress's feast on January 21.

Friday, July 29: Louis Martin dies at Saint-Sébastian-de Morsent, at La Musse.

Friday, September 14: Céline enters Lisieux Carmel.

1895

During the year: Thérèse writes Manuscript A.

Thursday, August 15: Thérèse's cousin Marie Guérin enters the Lisieux Carmel.

Thursday, October 17: Mother Agnes asks Thérèse to pray for Maurice Bellière, her first "spiritual brother."

1896

Monday, February 24: Profession of Sister Céline, Thérèse's sister.

Friday, April 3 (Good Friday): First hemoptysis, repeated in the evening.

Sunday, April 5 (Easter): Beginning of Thérèse's "trial of faith," which continues until her death.

Saturday, May 30: Mother Marie de Gonzague assigns Thérèse a second "spiritual brother," Adolphe Roulland.

Tuesday, September 8: Thérèse begins Manuscript B.

Saturday, November 21: Novena made for Thérèse's cure in hopes that she can eventually depart for a Carmel in Indochina; final relapse.

1897

Beginning of April: Thérèse falls seriously ill at the end of Lent.

Tuesday, April 6: Mother Agnes begins recording Thérèse's *Last Conversations*.

Thursday, June 3: Thérèse begins Manuscript C.

Thursday, July 8: Thérèse is transferred to the monastery infirmary.

Friday, July 30: Thérèse experiences continued hemoptyses and feelings of suffocation. At 6 P.M. she receives viaticum and extreme unction.

Thursday, September 30: Thérèse dies at about 7:20 P.M. Her final words are "My God, I love you."

Monday, October 4: Thérèse buried in the Lisieux cemetery.

1898 +1 yr.

September 30: 2,000 copies of *Story of a Soul* printed. A new edition is necessary each year thereafter.

1910 +12 y.

Beatification process opened.

1923 +13 y.

April 29: Thérèse beatified by Pius XI.

1925 +2 y.

May 17: Thérèse canonized by Pius XI in St. Peter's Basilica, Rome.

1980

June 2: John Paul II's pilgrimage to Lisieux.

✳Bibliography ✳

Writings

Sainte Thérèse de l'Enfant-Jésus et de la sainte-Face. *Oeuvres complètes*. Paris: Cerf-DDB, 1992.

Sainte Thérèse de l'Enfant-Jesus et de la sainte-Face. *Nouvelle édition du Centenaire*. 2d. ed. Paris: Cerf-DDB, 1992. Critical edition in eight volumes: 1. Manuscrits autobiographiques; 2. La première Histoire d'une âme (1898); 3. Correspondance générale I; 4. Correspondance générale II; 5. Poésies; 6. Recreations pieuses & Prieres; 7. Derniers entretiens; 8. Derniers paroles (synopsis).

François de Sainte-Marie. *Visage de Thérèse de Lisieux*. 2 vols. Lisieux: Office central de Lisieux, 1961. English language reprint edition: *The Photo Album of St. Thérèse of Lisieux*. Translated by Peter-Thomas

Rohrbach. Westminster, MD: Christian Classics, 1990.

Geneviève de la Saint-Face, *Conseils et Souvenirs*, Lisieux: 1952, 1973. English translation: *A Memoir of My Sister, St. Thérèse*. Translated by Carmelite Sisters of New York. New York: P. J. Kennedy & Sons, 1959.

Zélie Martin. *Correspondance familiale*. Lisieux: Office central de Lisieux, 1958.

Story of a Soul: The Autobiography of St. Thérèse of Lisieux. Translated by John Clarke. 3rd ed. Washington, DC: ICS Publications, 1996.

Letters of St. Thérèse of Lisieux: General Correspondence. Translated by John Clarke. 2 vols. Washington, DC: ICS Publications, 1982-1988.

The Poetry of Saint Thérèse of Lisieux. Translated by Donald Kinney. Washington, DC: ICS Publications, 1996.

The Plays of St. Thérèse of Lisieux: Pious Recreations. Translated by David Dwyer. Washington, DC: ICS Publications, 1997.

The Prayers of St. Thérèse of Lisieux. Translated by Aletheia Kane. Washington, DC: ICS Publications, 1997.

Thérèse of Lisieux: Her Last Conversations. Translated by John Clarke. Washington, DC: ICS Publications, 1977.

Biography and Analysis

Baudouin-Croix, Marie. *Léonie Martin: A Difficult Life*. Dublin: Veritas, 1993.

Bro. Bernard. *The Little Way: The Spirituality of Thérèse Of Lisieux*. Translated by Alan Neame. London: Darton, Longman and Todd, 1979.

————. *Thérèse de Lisieux: sa famille, son Dieu, son message*. Paris: Fayard, 1996.

Cadéot, Robert. *Louis Martin*. V.A.L., 1985.

Cadéot, Robert. *Zélie Martin*. V.A.L., 1990.

Chalon, Jean: *Thérèse de Lisieux: une vie d'amour*. Paris: Cerf, 1996.

Combes, Abbé André. *Collected Letters of Saint Thérèse of Lisieux*. Translated by F.J. Sheed. London: Sheed and Ward, 1949

Day, Dorothy. *Thérèse: A Life of Thérèse of Lisieux*. Reprint edition. Springfield, IL: Templegate Publishers, 1987.

D'Elbée, Jean du Coeur de Jésus. *I Believe in Love: Retreat Conferences on the Interior Life*. Chicago: Franciscan Herald Press, 1974.

De Meester, Conrad. *Dynamique de la confiance*. Paris: Cerf, 1995.

————. *With Empty Hands: the Message of Thérèse of Lisieux*. Homebush, New South Wales: St. Paul Publications, 1982; Tunbridge Wells; Burns and Oates, 1987.

————. *Saint Thérèse of Lisieux: Her Life, Times, and Teaching*. Washington, DC: ICS Publications, 1997.

Descouvemont, Pierre and Loose, Helmuth Nils. *Sainte Thérèse de Lisieux: la vie en images*. Paris: Cerf, 1995.

Descouvemont, Pierre and Loose, Helmuth Nils. *Thérèse and Lisieux*. Translated by Salvatore Sciurba. Grand Rapids, MI: Eerdmans, 1996.

Ducrocq, Marie-Pascale. *Thérèse of Lisieux: A Vocation Of Love*. Translated by Robert Jollett from 2nd edition. Staten Island, NY: Alba House, 1982.

Emert, Joyce. *Louis Martin: Father of a Saint*. Staten Island, NY: Alba House, 1983.

Frost, Christine. *A Guide to the Normandy of Saint Thérèse*. Birmingham: Theresian Trust, 1994.

————. *A Life of St Thérèse of Lisieux: The Little Flower.* Illustrated by Elizabeth Obbard. Wheathampstead, Hertfordshire: Anthony Clarke, 1988.

Gaucher, Guy. *The Passion of St. Thérèse of Lisieux.* New York: Crossroad, 1990.

————. *Saint Thérèse of Lisieux: From Lisieux to the Four Corners of the World.* Strasbourg: Editions du Signe, 1994.

————. *The Story of a Life: St. Thérèse of Lisieux.* San Francisco: Harper & Row, 1987.

Görres, Ida F. *The Hidden Face: A Study of St. Thérèse of Lisieux.* New York: Pantheon; London: Burns and Oates, 1959.

Hollings, Michael. *Thérèse of Lisieux: An Illustrated Life.* London: W. Collins & Co., 1981; Ann Arbor, MI: Servant Publications, 1991.

Jamart, François. *Complete Spiritual Doctrine of St. Thérèse of Lisieux.* New York: St. Paul Publications (Alba House), 1961.

Lafrance, Jean. *My Vocation is Love: Thérèse of Lisieux.* Translated by A.M. Brennan. Victoria, Australia, and Middlegreen, Slough, UK: St. Paul Publications, 1990.

Marie-Eugene of the Child Jesus. *Under the Torrent of his Love: Thérèse of Lisieux, a Spiritual Genius*. Staten Island, NY: Alba House, 1995.

O'Connor, Patricia. *In Search of Thérèse*. London: Darton, Longman & Todd; Wilmington, DE: Michael Glazier, 1987.

————. *Thérèse of Lisieux: A Biography*. Huntington, IN: Our Sunday Visitor, 1983.

O'Mahoney, Christopher, Translated by and ed. *Saint Thérèse of Lisieux by Those Who Knew Her: Testimonies from the process of Beatification*. Dublin. Veritas Publications, 1975, 1989; Huntington, IN: Our Sunday Visitor, 1976.

Piat, Stéphane-Joseph. *The Story of a Family: The Home Of the Little Flower*: Reprint edition. Rockford, IL: TAN Publications, 1995.

Redmond, Paulinus. *Louie and Zélie Martin: The Seed and the Root of the Little Flower*: London: Quiller Press, 1995.

Renault, Emmanuel. *L'épreuve de la foi: la combat de Thérèse de Lisieux*. Paris: Cerf-DDB, 1991.

Rohrbach, Peter-Thomas, *The Search for Saint Thérèse*. Garden City, NY: Doubleday and Co., 1961.

Six, Jean-François and Loose, Helmuth Nils. *Teresa di Lisieux*. Rome: Edizioni San Paolo, 1981.

Sullivan, John, ed. Carmelite Studies, vol. 5: *Experiencing St. Thérèse Today*. Washington, DC: ICS Publications, 1990.

Teresa Margaret. *I Choose All: A Study of St. Thérèse of Lisieux and Her Spiritual Doctrine*. Tenbury Wells, England: Fowler Wright Books, 1964.

Ulanov, Barry. *The Making of a Modern Saint: A Biographical Study of Thérèse of Lisieux*. Garden City, NY: Doubleday, 1996.

Vierge, Victor de la. *Spiritual Realism of Saint Thérèse of Lisieux: From the Original Manuscripts*. Milwaukee, WI: Bruce Publishing Co, 1961.

Vinatier, Jean. *Mère Agnès de Jésus*. Paris: Cerf, 1993.

Von Balthasar, Hans Urs. "Thérèse of Lisieux." In *Two Sisters in the Spirit: Thérèse of Lisieux and Elizabeth of the Trinity*, 13–362. San Francisco: Ignatius Press, 1992.

————. *Thérèse of Lisieux: The Story of a Mission*. Translated by Donald Nicholl. London, New York: Sheed and Ward, 1953.